A souvenir guide

# Queer City

## London Club Culture 1918–1967





**Note on terminology**: descriptive terms for LGBTQ+ people have changed over time, and many terms used in the historical records featured here are considered offensive today. In line with many contemporary scholars and community members, the authors of this text use the term 'queer' in its historical context and as an inclusive term to articulate the complex experiences of sexuality and gender diversity throughout history. In the text and images that follow we have also protected the identities of those individuals described in the files for data protection reasons. Therefore, first names or first initials are given rather than full family names.

Left Police photograph of the interior of the Caravan club, 1934. TNA: DPP2/224

Front cover Photograph of men and woman present at Fitzroy Square, 16th January 1927. TNA: CRIM 1/387

National Trust

The National Archives

# Queer City

## London Club Culture 1918–1967

Professor Matt Houlbrook, University of Birmingham

Above Police photograph of the interior of the Caravan club, 1934. TNA: DPP2/224

Right Detail of photograph of men and woman present at Fitzroy Square, 16th January 1927. TNA: CRIM 1/387

In January 1927, Bill scribbled a note to his "Honey Bunch" to make plans for the coming weekend: "I will be outside Lees Hall at 8 o'clock on Saturday and we can easily find a dance." Excited at the prospect of a night out together, Bill ended his letter with a reminder. "We have fixed nothing for Saturday yet but there are plenty of dances so don't forget to come." There was nothing unusual about this. By 1927, at the height of the 1920s dancing craze, London's nightlife offered countless opportunities to dance. In fashionable nightclubs, suburban Palais de Danse, and church halls and workingmen's clubs, men and women could Charleston to the latest jazz music. Bill's lover, however – to whom he signed off "Cheerio 'my love'" – was a young man called Bert.

Think about that. Over ninety years ago – forty years before the Sexual Offences Act partially decriminalised sex between men – two young men were confident they could find somewhere to dance together on a Saturday night. Bill and Bert's plans challenge all of our preconceptions about the queer past. A crumpled handwritten letter evokes possibilities for living and loving that, we are often told, only emerged after the moment of Gay Liberation in the early 1970s.

We do not know where Bill and Bert went that weekend. They were probably among the crowds on the ballroom floor of the Adelphi Rooms, on Edgware Road, during the winter of 1926–7, however. Leslie Kinder, the waiter who hired the hall for fortnightly dances, was friends with Bert. Having paid six guineas to the hall's owners, he sold tickets for two shillings and sixpence to friends and acquaintances on the door or by post. By December 1926, these popular events were attracting up to 300 men – clerks, cabinet makers, a coach painter – many of whom were "painted and powdered… [wearing]

earrings and low necked dresses." And the Adelphi Rooms were not the only place same-sex couples gathered and danced in the 1920s and 1930s. The venues changed all the time, but London's extensive queer scene included nightclubs like the Caravan, in Endell Street, Billie's, in Little Denmark Street, and Betty's in Archer Street.

Not everyone knew about such places; not everyone could afford the admission fee. Yet with knowledge and money nightclubs and dance halls provided enticing opportunities – social and sexual, personal and political. In a period when the more public world of streets, cafes, and urinals could carry considerable dangers, here was a quasi-private world in which to relax, meet friends, have fun, and know that one was not alone. In Billie's club, one night in 1937, an observer overheard an intimate conversation between two friends:

> "You do look worried tonight darling, whatever is the matter with you?" … "My sweetie has let me down, he promised to come to my flat this evening and I waited in for him. He didn't even phone me the darling bitch. I feel so lonely now."

For those let down in love, there was consolation in companionship. As the piano played in the Caravan's stifling hot basement, far from work and the streets above, men were "dancing together… pausing to caress each other's buttocks …go[ing] through the motions of sexual intercourse… embracing and kissing." Temporarily, perhaps, the constraints of everyday life no longer applied.

Cyril Coeur de Leon was one of the Caravan's regular visitors. It was here that he made friends and embarked on a series of passionate affairs. It was here that he found himself. Writing to Billy, one of the club's owners, in 1934, Cyril reflected on his relationships, his feelings, and his new life in the city. He wrote "I have only been queer since I came to London about two years ago, before then I knew nothing about it." Even now, Cyril's excitement at the world he had found – its importance in his life – is tangible.

Far from clandestine, venues like the Adelphi Rooms were tightly woven into the fabric of London's commercial nightlife. This vibrant social world did not exist on the margins of urban life, but was an integral part of it. At times queer venues became strikingly visible parts of neighbourhood life. Flyers for the Caravan circulated around Seven Dials and Soho; posters for the "Hotel Staff Dances" held in Holland Park Avenue did the rounds in west London. Dancing's popularity echoed the leisure fashions of the 1920s and 1930s. At the same time as Leslie Kinder's events, the Adelphi Rooms hosted Elsie French's "Grand Dance," the Irish Clan Na' Heirran's St Patrick's Day Ball, and the Jamaican Laurie French's dances for West Indian and West African men and white women. The same venue, dancing, and soundtrack – "Syncopated Jazz aces."

Same-sex couples thus often shared the dance floor with other groups. Exclusive venues were few and far between until after the Second World War. The Caravan's "cosmopolitan" character was not a straightforward code word for queer but signalled a venue in which visitors of all sorts and conditions mixed. The geography of club cultures tracked that of London's nightlife in general. The Caravan drew much of its ambience from its location in Seven Dials. This cosmopolitan working-class neighbourhood, on the borders of the expanding theatre district and Covent Garden markets, was an appropriate home for an excitingly shabby basement club. It existed alongside rough-and-ready pubs, Italian and Jewish refreshment houses, and the cafe where Jim and Emily Kitten served rice and curries to sailors, students, and musicians – like Laurie French – from across the empire.

These opportunities were underpinned by money. At least some entrepreneurs found lucrative business in running venues where men and women might freely dance and socialise. Shady estate agents specialised in letting premises in Soho and Seven Dials for nightclubs. When William Reynolds was looking to invest a recent inheritance of £300, he partnered up with the notorious West End character Jack Neave – "Iron Foot Jack" – and rented an Endell Street basement. What became the Caravan built on Neave's experience running similar clubs and sought to recoup their investment by charging one shilling and sixpence. Of Selina Hopps's Baker Street establishment, one observer noted: she "knew the sort of people who frequented the place and by gathering them in large numbers… was making considerable profits."

The boundaries between profit and politics – commerce and community – were never clear. Leslie Kinder never really made any money from his events at the Adelphi Rooms. Around 1932 "Lady Austin" and John Packer ran a series of spectacular drag balls in a Holland Park Avenue ballroom. This was not for financial reward, but "only for our love for each other." When the premises was raided by police, the experience of personal affirmation and collective identity – love – played out as a dramatic and radical political intervention. "Surely in a free country we can do what we like?" David M. asked the detective arresting him. "We know each other and are doing no harm… I am afraid a few will have to suffer yet before our ways are made legal." At this moment of crisis, Lady Austin also spoke back:

> "There is nothing wrong in [what we do]. You may think so but it is what we call real love man for man. You call us Nancies and bum boys but… before long our cult will be allowed in this country."

Here was an outspoken demand for reform of the sexual offences laws, made not in a Home Office committee room, but on a dance floor in West London.

Here is an important reminder: making money and living and loving brought the people who made London's club cultures into precarious relation with its police and the courts. Venues like Billie's were never 'illegal' in any straightforward sense. Their legal status and organisation made nightclubs safer than the cafes or pubs where men and women also met; they were worlds apart from cottages and cruising grounds. Yet at different times, provisions on liquor or dancing licensing and legislation on "keeping a disorderly house" and "corrupting public morals" could be used against the proprietors and habitués of queer venues. Raids on nightclubs were not regular, but happened enough to make a point. Observed quietly by plainclothes detectives for several weeks, the Adelphi Rooms was raided at the end of 1926. Leslie Kinder was sentenced to 21 months in prison. That Christmas he wrote sadly to Bobby B, Bert's housemate: "I think it is somewhat unkind not to have wrote me."

What the *News of the World* called "Grave Dance Hall Scandals" were followed in the early 1930s by a string of sensational "pansy cases." Pressured by organisations like the Public Morality Council, police raided clubs like the Caravan – arresting up to 100 people at a time. The ensuing trials were front page news. Proprietors and frequenters appeared in court, identified by numbered placards around their necks, and were subjected to punitive penal sentences and vitriolic judicial comments. The longest sentences were reserved for the nightclub owners. Other men, however, went to prison for a month or three simply because they were on the premises when police arrived. Wearing make-up or dancing with another man apparently constituted the shared responsibility necessary to be convicted of "aiding and abetting in keeping a disorderly house."

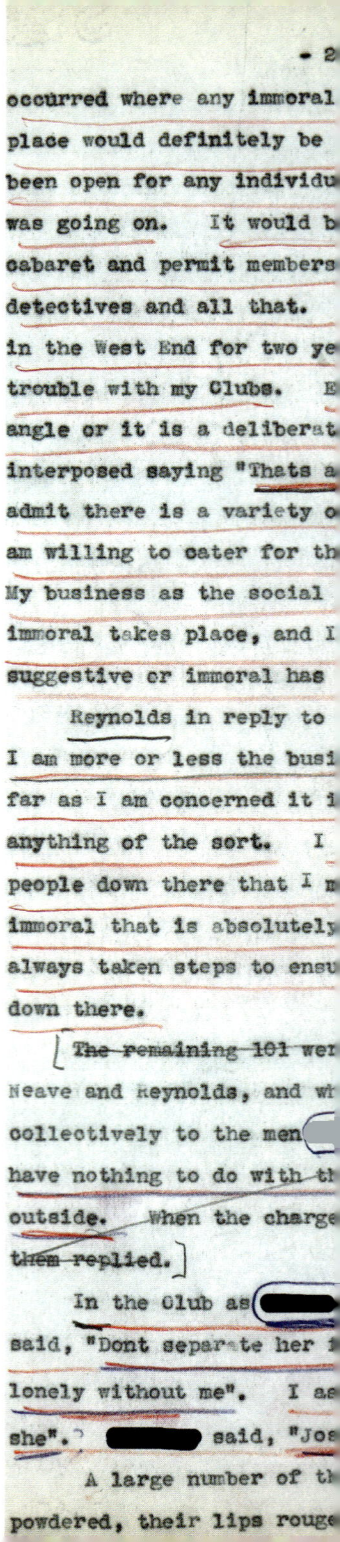
- 2
occurred where any immoral
place would definitely be
been open for any individu
was going on. It would b
cabaret and permit members
detectives and all that.
in the West End for two ye
trouble with my Clubs. E
angle or it is a deliberat
interposed saying "Thats a
admit there is a variety o
am willing to cater for th
My business as the social
immoral takes place, and I
suggestive or immoral has
Reynolds in reply to
I am more or less the busi
far as I am concerned it i
anything of the sort. I
people down there that I m
immoral that is absolutely
always taken steps to ensu
down there.
[The remaining 101 wer
Neave and Reynolds, and wh
collectively to the men
have nothing to do with th
outside. When the charge
them replied.]
In the Club as
said, "Dont separate her f
lonely without me". I as
she". said, "Jos
A large number of th
powdered, their lips rouge

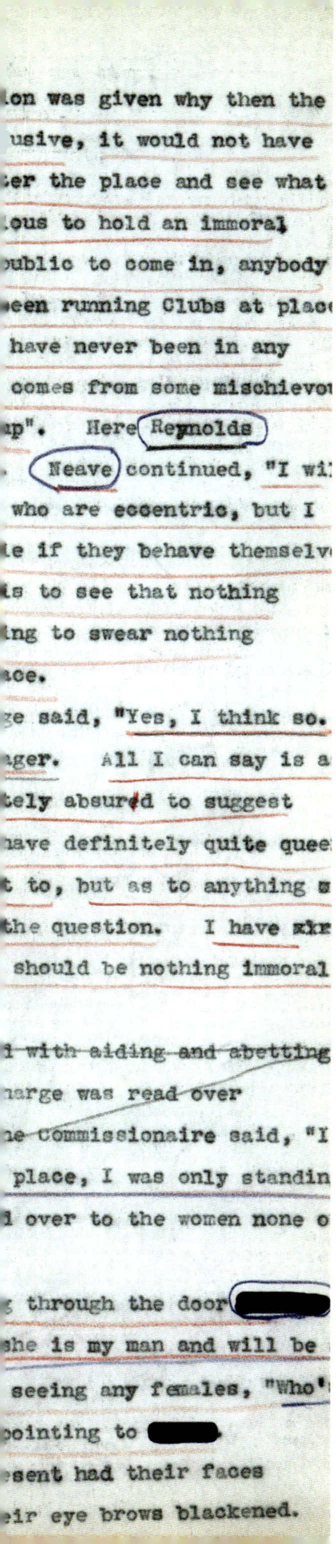
ion was given why then the
usive, it would not have
ter the place and see what
ous to hold an immoral
public to come in, anybody
een running Clubs at plac
have never been in any
comes from some mischievo
p". Here Reynolds
Neave continued, "I wi
who are eccentric, but I
e if they behave themselv
is to see that nothing
ng to swear nothing
ace.
e said, "Yes, I think so.
ger. All I can say is a
tely absurd to suggest
have definitely quite quee
t to, but as to anything
the question. I have
should be nothing immoral
l with aiding and abetting
harge was read over
e Commissionaire said, "I
place, I was only standin
l over to the women none o
through the door
she is my man and will be
seeing any females, "Who'
pointing to
esent had their faces
eir eye brows blackened.

The troubling paradox of the historical record: most of what we know about these vibrant club cultures comes from those who tried to suppress them. We hear a couple talking because a plainclothes detective listened in; we see men dancing together because it was described in courtroom evidence; we look into a basement club through a police photographer's lens.

How else do you think I know what Bill wrote to Bert in January 1927? Bert was arrested, his letters confiscated; aged 17 he went to prison for eight months.

The comedy of the historical record: policemen always looked for evidence to secure a conviction under licensing regulations or for keeping a disorderly house. This meant their reports often did not record the presence of women dancing together in a nightclub, but instead provided meticulous records of the contents of a glass.

Bert and Bill's confidence challenges how we think about the chronology of the queer past. This history is not a linear story of "progress" or "liberation." The opportunities the men enjoyed reflected a social world that was perhaps more extensive and vibrant than at any point before the late-1960s. The "pansy cases" of the 1930s, expansion of police powers during the Second World War, and a growing focus on using licensing regulations against proprietors transformed London's nightclubs. By the late-1940s, the most successful venues were discreet, private, and invisible. Increasingly now run by and for queer men, the need to stay on the right side of the law meant they carefully policed their customer's behaviour. Places like Stan Cowley's Arts and Battledress Club – opened in Orange Street in 1941, before moving to Rupert Street in 1952 – stayed open for several decades. They did so through a rigid door policy, high membership fees, and strict dress codes. Until a new generation of coffee houses and discos emerged in the 1960s and 1970s, it often seemed inconceivable that men had ever been able to dance together in central London.

Bill's letter to his "Honey Bunch" evoked a world that is now long gone. We can see the Holland Park Avenue house where "Lady Austin's Camp Boys" gathered. The Adelphi Rooms has been demolished, however. Like all such venues, its presence in London's commercial landscape was transient – however colourful Leslie Kinder's dances might have been. How do we mark sites like this? Memories and histories are embedded in place. So, too, are the contemporary communities that they sustain. Bill's letter offers a challenge: bringing London's club cultures back to life – even if it does mean working through a police photographer's lens – is history as politics.

Left Statement by Divisional Detective Inspector Clarence, 1934. TNA: DPP2/224

Right Handbill advertising a ball for 'hotel staff' taken as evidence, 1933. TNA: CRIM 1/638

# Queer Collections, Queer Spaces

Rowena Hillel and Victoria Iglikowski,
The National Archives

"I have only been queer since I came to London… before then I knew nothing about it."

This surprisingly open expression of a queer identity and its link to London is found in a letter written in 1934 housed at The National Archives. The author of the letter, Cyril Coeur de Leon, would have to wait a further 33 years before the passing of the 1967 Sexual Offences Act, which finally decriminalised homosexual acts in private in England and Wales. 2017 marks the 50th anniversary of the passing of the Act and the 60th anniversary of the Wolfenden Report, which recommended decriminalisation.

The National Archives' collections, including Metropolitan Police files, give a valuable insight into how the state played a major role in

Left: Map of Hyde Park showing areas of 'immorality', 1937. TNA: WORK16/543

repressing and controlling the lives of queer men and women. These collections include the original government correspondence leading up to the passing of the 1967 Act and evidence collected for the Wolfenden Committee. Many of these records are characterised by a surprising openness around sexuality in a time before homosexual acts were decriminalised.

While it was never actually illegal to be gay, the police criminalised certain social, cultural and sexual practices. Expanding on previous acts, Section 11 of the 1885 Criminal Law Amendment Act, the notorious Labouchére Amendment, criminalised "gross indecency". This law, under which Oscar Wilde was sentenced, included all sexual acts between men short of, and including, "sodomy", committed in public or in private. In the eyes of the law meeting other men could be deemed as soliciting and running a club could be seen as running a brothel or "disorderly house". In just going about their daily lives men could be arrested, prosecuted, whipped and imprisoned for up to ten years.

As well as criminalisation, homosexuality was widely deemed socially unacceptable. Public exposure in the press could mean exclusion from friends and family and dismissal from work. Blackmail was commonplace. Some chose to commit suicide rather than risk being found out.

Despite persistent targeting and surveillance throughout 1918–1967 there was a thriving queer community who were able and willing to socialise despite the risk. Men were able to create both public and private spaces to meet other men, socialise and have relationships. These queer spaces could be found in urinals, pubs, restaurants, dancehalls, clubs, houses, furnished rooms and Turkish baths.

Many of the records held at The National Archives reflect the importance of London in enabling these spaces to thrive. The West End was a particularly important hub and from the 1930s a number of queer-friendly private members' clubs appeared. Some proprietors simply accepted gay men's customs; others deliberately cultivated a queer clientele. Most were not queer run, but offered the possibility of protection and a "safe space". Many of the underground spaces also welcomed migrants, prostitutes and bohemians, who were collectively deemed outsiders in this era.

In these spaces gay men could find partners on the street without being detected, by means of a simple look or a gesture. By experience and via gossip and stories reported in the press they learned how to avoid surveillance. Coded love letters and frequently used pseudonyms, found in amongst the police files, point to clever tactics used by the queer community to avoid persecution.

Furthermore, as the records indicate, Metropolitan Police officers were remarkably reluctant to act formally, often doing so in response to public complaints. This reluctance to act was fuelled by continuing controversy over undercover police methods used to catch out gay men, and public outcry at the "moral corruption" of the police officers involved.

The experience of surveillance differed depending on class, race, age, gender and place. There was far greater risk of being caught in a urinal in the West End than a private room in the East. The examples of queer spaces in The National Archives' records represent a selection of prominent clubs that were made examples of by the police. These cases demonstrate the police association of being queer with certain characteristics and behaviour. Many individuals in the records cross-dressed and wore make-up, for example. This was seen by the police as a sign

Charge of gross indecency, Pope's Lane public urinals, Brixton, 1932.
TNA: CRIM 1/617

Right Locations of urinals where arrests were made during 1953, submitted as evidence as part of the 1957 Wolfenden report. TNA: HO 345/7

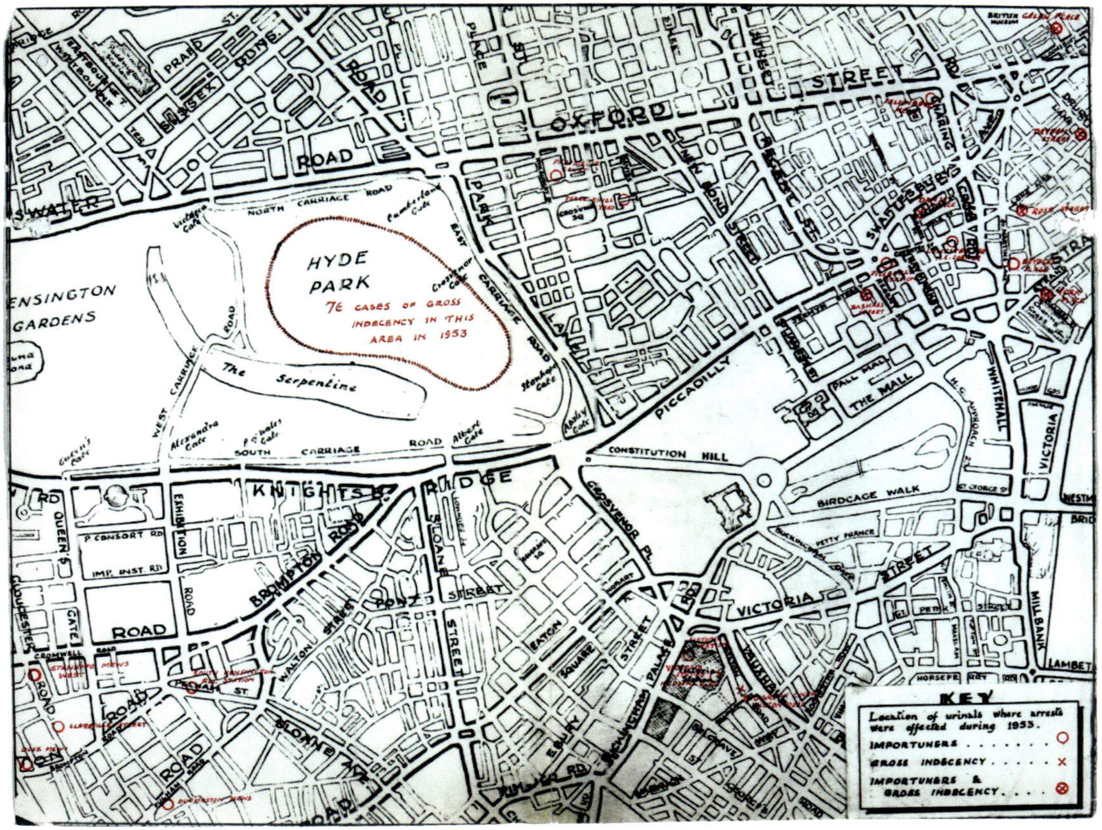

of homosexuality. Paradoxically, queer men who did not fit the police stereotype could carry out their lives and relationships relatively undetected by police surveillance.

Equally, because it was never illegal for a woman to have a relationship with another woman (sex was seen from the male perspective as needing penetration), there are far fewer records relating to lesbian relationships. But lesbianism was not socially acceptable either and in amongst files dealing with homosexual acts there are references to lesbians in both the police records and letters from the public.

Throughout 1918–1967 thousands of men were arrested and imprisoned for carrying out homosexual acts. Thousands more were the victims of press exposure, blackmail, and ostracisation from society. The records of The National Archives offer a snap-shot of LGBTQ+ experiences and the ways in which the state attempted to control and regulate such activity. The files and letters which tell Cyril's story and the many others held in The National Archives demonstrate the importance of specifically queer spaces in the context of a time when people didn't always have safe access to such spaces. These records can play a key role in re-examining traditional historical narratives and bringing marginalised histories to the fore.

# 25 Fitzroy Square, Fitzrovia

A rented basement flat at 25 Fitzroy Square was the home of Robert, a dancer in the "Lady Be Good" chorus at the Empire Theatre who was known as "Bobby B". The flat was also the venue for hedonistic parties throughout the mid-1920s. During these parties Bobby B and his male friends would dance and sing together, and occasionally even have sex. According to police reports they were flamboyantly open about their sexuality, wearing powdered makeup and dressing in ladies' shoes.

Private residences like Bobby B's were important spaces for queer men to meet and socialise, providing an alternative to the underground clubs. Opportunities to visit places like these were often initiated through networks of friends. In one report Bobby notes:

> "Some of the men I have known for a long time and they bring along any of their friends if they care to do so."

Due to restrictions on police entering some buildings without a warrant, they had to rely on reports from people concerned about illegal homosexual acts being carried out in private rooms. Fitzroy Square came to the attention of local police after they received information concerning indecent and immoral behaviour going on outside the premises. Over several nights in the winter of 1926/7 Sergeant Arthur observed the men entering and leaving Bobby B's flat. His observations led the police to conclude that Fitzroy Square was the resort of what were known as "Nancy Boys".

> "At 11:45pm I saw two men who I saw enter at 11:30pm leave; they were undoubtedly men of the Nancy type. They walked cuddling one another to Tottenham Court Road, where they stood waiting for a bus. I stood close to them and saw their faces were powdered and painted and their appearance and manner strongly suggested them to be importuners of men."

At 1am on the 16th January 1927, armed with a newly issued warrant, Superintendent George and accompanying officers approached Fitzroy Square to arrest the occupants inside. Superintendent George describes the raid that followed:

> "I found a red light burning over the area door, downstairs from the street. I knocked and the prisoner [Constance] opened. I told her we were police officers and held a warrant to arrest her. Chief inspector S read the warrant. She said 'That is not true. [Bobby B] was going to give us a Salome dance'. In the front of the room we saw the prisoner [Bobby B]. He was wearing a thin black transparent skirt, with gilt trimming round the edge and a red sash that was tied round his loins. He wore lady shoes and was naked from the loins upwards."

The Salome dance Constance refers to held particular significance to the police. The dance originated from Oscar Wilde's play of the same name, and was considered erotic and highly

Right Police Sketch of Fitzroy Square, 1927. TNA: CRIM 1/387

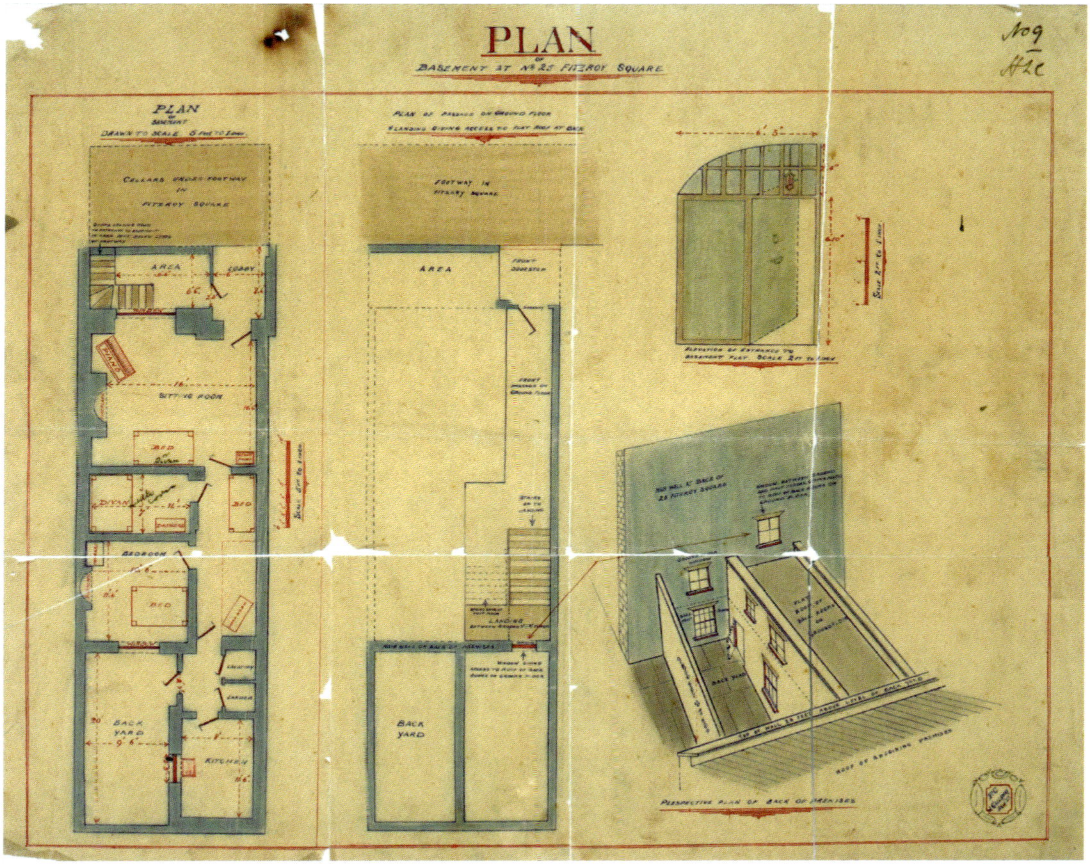


controversial due to it involving nudity. Such a performance confirmed to the police that the occupants were acting in an indecent and immoral fashion.

Whilst inside the flat, the police took photographs to be used later in the trial. These offer a rare snapshot of the men and woman present during the raid. Names scribbled above the photographs link to those mentioned in the witness statements.

The image over leaf shows some of the guests standing together in the front room of the flat. Two of the guests have their eyes closed, while two look away. Bobby B is wearing the Salome dancing costume referenced in the police statements. The association between suggested effeminate behaviour and homosexuality is clear; these behaviours were exaggerated in the trial to highlight Bobby's deviation from perceived sexual norms.

The judge concluded that Fitzroy Square was a "disorderly house" because it was "not regulated by the constraints of morality", mentioning "disgusting practices (sodomy)... tippling, whoring, using obscene language... and behaving in a lewd, obscene and disorderly manner". Bobby B and Constance were charged with maintaining a disorderly house and Bobby was sentenced to 15 months hard labour in prison. In the eyes of the police, this served as a clear

Above Photograph of men and woman present at Fitzroy Square, 16th January 1927. TNA: CRIM 1/387

warning to any men considering frequenting such an establishment in the future.

Alongside the photographs and witness statements, the police file contains a number of letters that were found during the raid and used as evidence. These letters, especially one from Bert to his "Honey bunch" Bill, hint at the thriving queer scene in 1920s London:

> "I will be outside Lees Hall at 8 o'c on Saturday and we can easily find a dance. There is always St. Michaels of course."

Other letters reveal the dangers of carrying out a queer relationship in a society that condemns homosexuality. A poignant letter, addressed to "Peter darling" by his lover Eric, highlights the continuing pressure to hide his sexuality from his family and colleagues:

> "I might be able (if father isn't with me) to call for you about 7:30 or so and take you along, if you would care for a ride, and then we can fool around until the meeting is over, when we would have to pick up the old boy again, but it's very doubtful. If you feel at all inclined to come, just wait further news, which I will get to you by hook or crook, but be prepared to be let down. I'm ever so sorry darling, as you know I would do everything for an extra evening with you, but you see how things are don't you? ... Thank you Peter boy for ringing me up. Your voice sounded wonderful, and I wanted to shout out to all the office and come and tell them that I was in love with you. What a good job I restrained myself, wasn't it. I'm sorry I couldn't say anything more to you but the room was full up with people."

Another particularly striking letter from Eric to Bert describes an unrequited love:

> "You say that you could never love me, but that you offer me friendship, which you say is far greater than love. I cannot agree with you about this my dear... I must confess that I don't see how I can keep love out of my side of the friendship. It is a simple true fact that I love you baby dear."

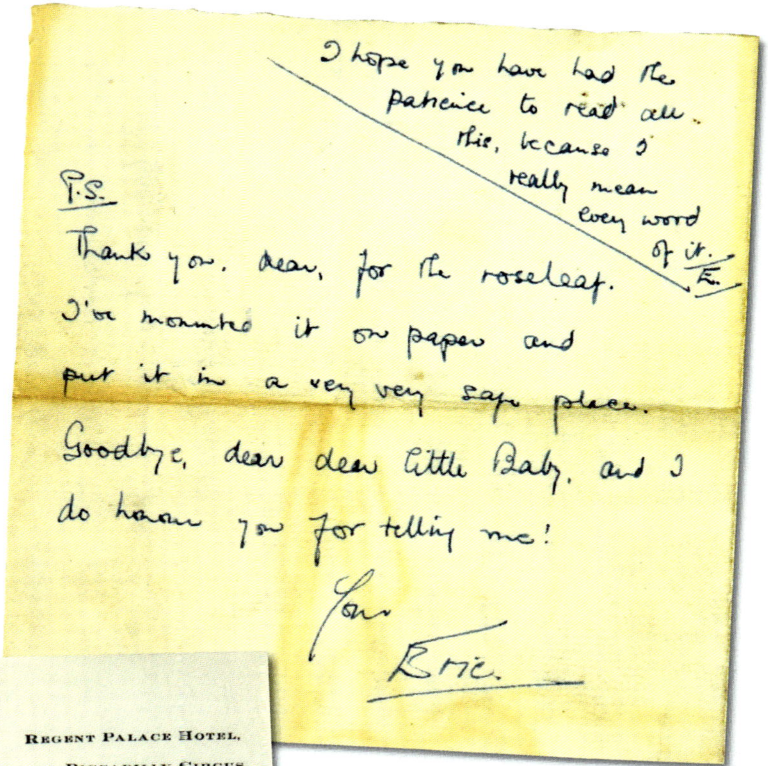

I hope you have had the patience to read all this, because I really mean every word of it. E.

P.S.

Thank you, dear, for the roseleaf. I've mounted it on paper and put it in a very very safe place.

Goodbye, dear dear little Baby, and I do honour you for telling me!

Yours

Eric.

Below Letter from Eric to Peter, found at Fitzroy Square, 16th January 1927. TNA: CRIM 1/387

Right Letter from Eric to Peter, found at Fitzroy Square, 16th January 1927. TNA: CRIM 1/387

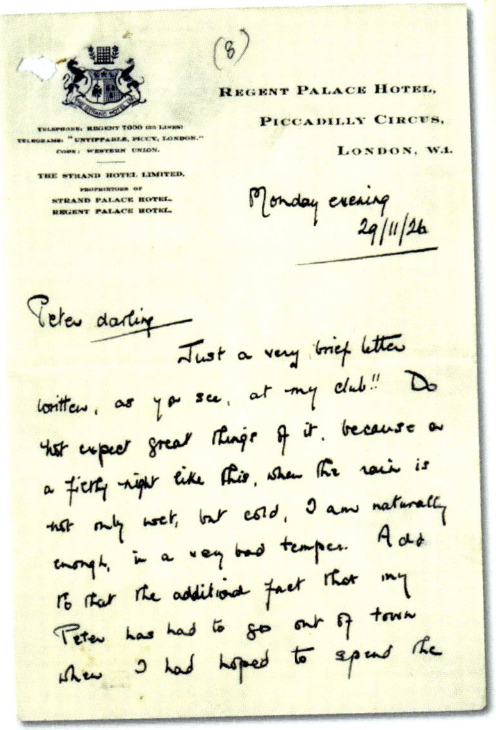

(8)

REGENT PALACE HOTEL,
PICCADILLY CIRCUS,
LONDON, W.1.

TELEPHONE: REGENT 7000 (35 LINES)
TELEGRAMS: "UNTIPPABLE, PICCY, LONDON."
CODE: WESTERN UNION.

THE STRAND HOTEL LIMITED,
PROPRIETORS OF
STRAND PALACE HOTEL,
REGENT PALACE HOTEL.

Monday evening
29/11/26

Peter darling

Just a very brief letter written, as you see, at my club!! Do not expect great things of it, because on a filthy night like this, when the rain is not only wet, but cold, I am naturally enough, in a very bad temper. Add to that the additional fact that my Peter has had to go out of town when I had hoped to spend the

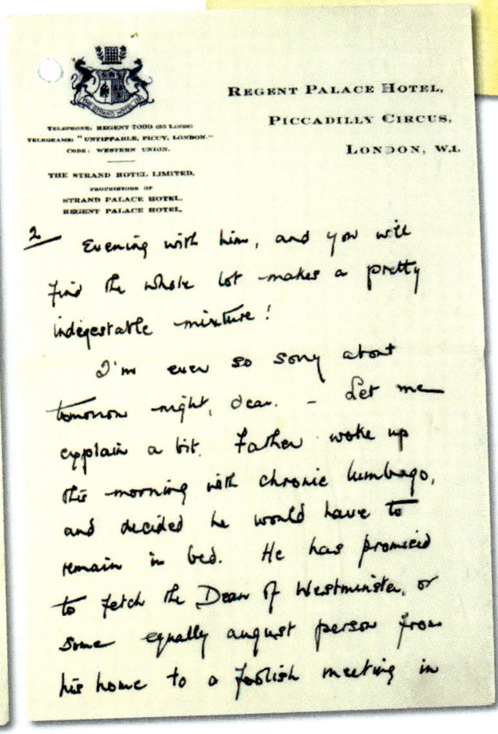

REGENT PALACE HOTEL,
PICCADILLY CIRCUS,
LONDON, W.1.

TELEPHONE: REGENT 7000 (35 LINES)
TELEGRAMS: "UNTIPPABLE, PICCY, LONDON."
CODE: WESTERN UNION.

THE STRAND HOTEL LIMITED,
PROPRIETORS OF
STRAND PALACE HOTEL,
REGENT PALACE HOTEL.

2 evening with him, and you will find the whole lot makes a pretty indigestible mixture!

I'm ever so sorry about tomorrow night, dear. – Let me explain a bit. Father woke up this morning with chronic lumbago, and decided he would have to remain in bed. He has promised to fetch the Dean of Westminster, or some equally august person from his home to a foolish meeting in

The use of these personal love letters as evidence by police demonstrates the very real danger of practising homosexuality in the 1920s. However, the open declarations of love and friendship shown within the letters highlight the continued resilience of men like Peter, Eric and Bert to be sexually open, despite the risks. Bobby B's basement flat at Fitzroy Square was one of many queer spaces providing such an opportunity.

# Shim Sham Club, Soho

Queer club culture in the 1930s was vibrant and varied, especially in the growing post-First World War underground scene. Music was central to the character of many of these venues, from the music hall artists of Billie's Club to the expanding London jazz scene.

Particularly prominent amongst these unlicensed clubs was the Shim Sham, a queer-friendly jazz club described in Metropolitan Police records as a "den of vice and iniquity". The club originally opened in 1935 on Wardour Street in the heart of Soho, and from that point on it constantly attracted police attention. The club was heavily associated with African American culture, the name of the venue itself taken from the shim sham dance – a lively tap dance originating in Harlem.

The Shim Sham gained its notoriety with the police due to its policy on the sale of alcohol. Similar to many other clubs of 1930s London, the Shim Sham tried to avoid liquor licensing regulations by running as a so-called "bottle party". Indeed *The Daily Express* described it as the "first bottle party in London". Such unlicensed clubs attempted to evade the law by claiming to run as a private party and offering alcohol on the basis that it was pre-ordered through wine merchants. This essentially avoided the restrictions of conventional licensing hours, aiming to attract punters around the clock. Metropolitan Police records show concern in the rapid increase in bottle parties operating during this era, with a steady rise from 1934 onwards. On 5th July 1935 undercover police first

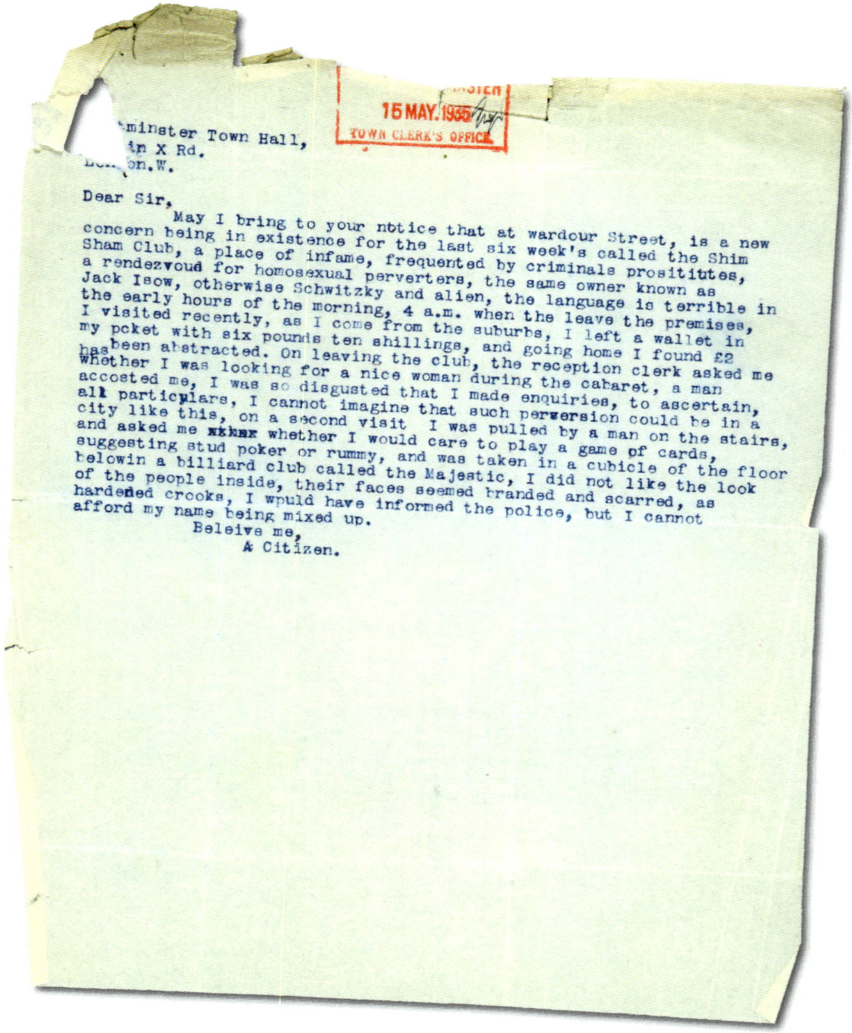
15 MAY. 1935
TOWN CLERK'S OFFICE

minster Town Hall,
in X Rd.
London.W.

Dear Sir,

May I bring to your nbtice that at wardour Street, is a new concern being in existence for the last six week's called the Shim Sham Club, a place of infame, frequented by criminals prosititutes, a rendezvoud for homosexual perverters, the same owner known as Jack Isow, otherwise Schwitzky and alien, the language is terrible in the early hours of the morning, 4 a.m. when the leave the premises, I visited recently, as I come from the suburbs, I left a wallet in my pcket with six pounds ten shillings, and going home I found £2 has been abstracted. On leaving the club, the reception clerk asked me whether I was looking for a nice woman during the cabaret, a man accosted me, I was so disgusted that I made enquiries, to ascertain, all particulars, I cannot imagine that such perversion could be in a city like this, on a second visit I was pulled by a man on the stairs, and asked me whether I would care to play a game of cards, suggesting stud poker or rummy, and was taken in a cubicle of the floor belowin a billiard club called the Majestic, I did not like the look of the people inside, their faces seemed branded and scarred, as hardened crooks, I wpuld have informed the police, but I cannot afford my name being mixed up.

Beleive me,

A Citizen.

Left Letter of complaint about the Shim Sham, signed "A Citizen", 1935. TNA: MEPO 2/4494

3 JUL 1947

I.B. 112

APPLIC… TRAVEL DOCUMENT

FOR ALIENS W… AT AN EARLY DATE AND FOR WHOM … TS ARE NOT AVAILABLE

This form, when … .M. Chief Inspector, Immigration Branch, Home Office, 10, Old Bailey … all unmounted recent passport photographs of the applicant and wi… ed by a responsible person, the Police Registration Certificate/s … accompanying, any former passports or travel documents and the p… ........ Fees should be paid by Postal Order and made payable to the Accounting Officer, Home Office, and crossed. (Cheques cannot be accepted.)

Date 27/6/47 Fee Stamp No. 1929 30507 (For Official Use.)

Surname (In capital letters) ISOWITZSKY alias ISOW.

Forename(s) JOSEPH AARON

Accompanied by wife* and ........ Child (Children)*. * Strike out if not applicable.

Place and Date of Birth CABILAER RUSSIA. 21/1/99

Occupation CATERER Married or Single MARRIED

Present Residence 11 STRATHMORE COURT PARK RD. N.W.8.

Right Photograph of Shim Sham owner Jack Isow, 1947. TNA: HO 405/24361

raided the premises on the grounds of liquor licence evasion, and the venue was charged with operating as an unlicensed club.

## "A den of vice and iniquity."

While the venue was investigated for offences of liquor licensing, the club's associations with black music artists, progressive politics and same-sex relationships also attracted significant attention.

Public letters were repeatedly sent to police raising concerns around the morals of the club. A local resident wrote to the Police Commissioner signing themselves as "a neighbour of Wardour Street" complaining that "In the Shim Sham there is a negro band, white women carrying on perversion, women with women, men with men, a second Caravan Club." These letters capture the wider social atmosphere of the era, and even though same-sex relationships between women were not criminal, they demonstrate public disapproval. Anonymous aliases, such as "An Englishman", "A Citizen" and "pro bono publico", the Latin phrase meaning "for the public good", attempted to take a moral high ground, drawing on themes of race, class and civic duty.

The letter signed by "A Citizen" declares the Shim Sham to be a "rendezvous for homosexual perverts", but the author goes on to make a return visit to the club.

As well as the interest in queer relations taking place in the club, the interracial relationships caused controversy. The venue took the position of welcoming both black and white patrons. A police report by Stannard from June 1935 noted "there was also about 20 coloured men present dancing with white women. Many of the persons present were drunk and I recognised many of the women present as prostitutes." One letter noted

Below Menu from the Shim Sham Cabaret, taken as police evidence in relation to unregistered clubs, bottle parties and sale of liquor out of hours, 1935–1938.
TNA: MEPO 2/4494

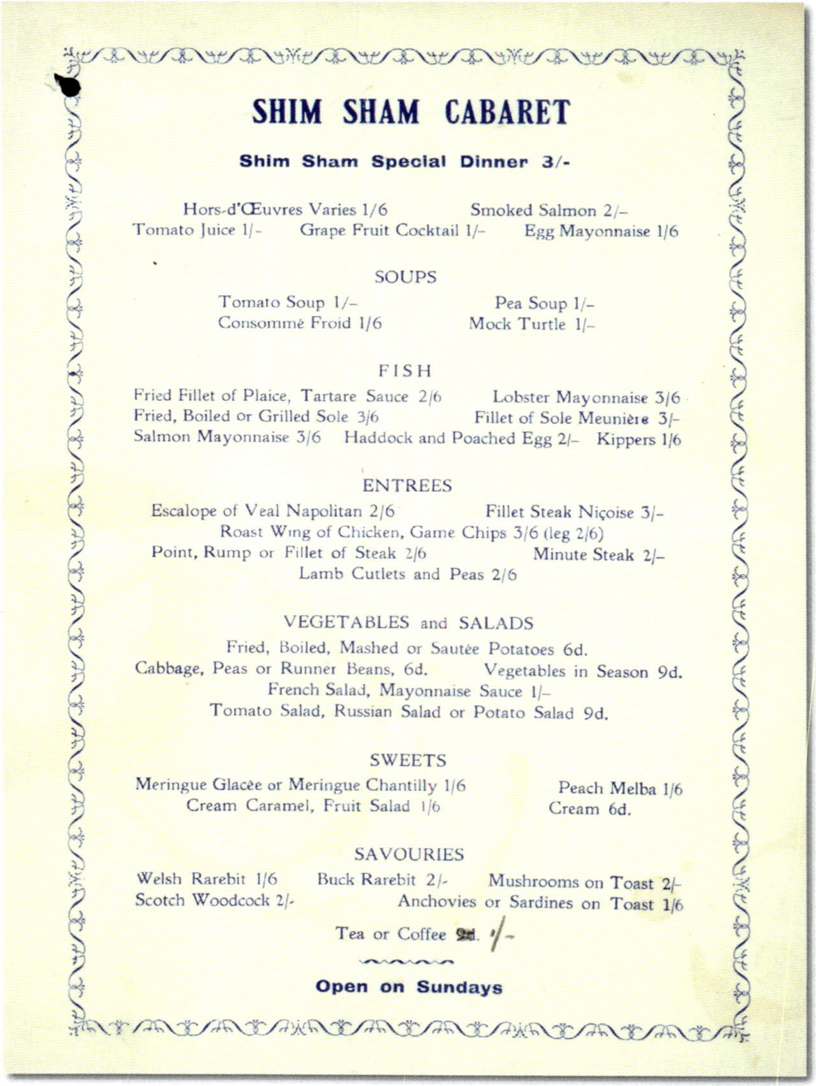

SHIM SHAM CABARET

Shim Sham Special Dinner 3/-

Hors-d'Œuvres Varies 1/6 — Smoked Salmon 2/–
Tomato Juice 1/– — Grape Fruit Cocktail 1/– — Egg Mayonnaise 1/6

SOUPS

Tomato Soup 1/– — Pea Soup 1/–
Consommé Froid 1/6 — Mock Turtle 1/–

FISH

Fried Fillet of Plaice, Tartare Sauce 2/6 — Lobster Mayonnaise 3/6
Fried, Boiled or Grilled Sole 3/6 — Fillet of Sole Meunière 3/–
Salmon Mayonnaise 3/6 — Haddock and Poached Egg 2/– — Kippers 1/6

ENTREES

Escalope of Veal Napolitan 2/6 — Fillet Steak Niçoise 3/–
Roast Wing of Chicken, Game Chips 3/6 (leg 2/6)
Point, Rump or Fillet of Steak 2/6 — Minute Steak 2/–
Lamb Cutlets and Peas 2/6

VEGETABLES and SALADS

Fried, Boiled, Mashed or Sautée Potatoes 6d.
Cabbage, Peas or Runner Beans, 6d. — Vegetables in Season 9d.
French Salad, Mayonnaise Sauce 1/–
Tomato Salad, Russian Salad or Potato Salad 9d.

SWEETS

Meringue Glacée or Meringue Chantilly 1/6 — Peach Melba 1/6
Cream Caramel, Fruit Salad 1/6 — Cream 6d.

SAVOURIES

Welsh Rarebit 1/6 — Buck Rarebit 2/- — Mushrooms on Toast 2/–
Scotch Woodcock 2/- — Anchovies or Sardines on Toast 1/6

Tea or Coffee ~~9d.~~ 1/-

Open on Sundays

"the encouraging of Black and White intercourse is the talk of the West End". The public letters seem to align perceived sexual "deviance" with the varied ethnicities of the clientele. Such letters increased police interest in these venues.

As well as the diverse clientele, the owners also attracted scrutiny. Jack Isow, known as "Flash Isow", was a Polish Jew born in Russia. The Shim Sham was said to be bringing him £100 a week in profit. This was far from Isow's only interaction with the police; he was later associated with gambling, police bribery and black market food-selling. The other owner was the African American singer Ike Hatch, who performed at the club and appears to have commissioned the music.

## "London's miniature Harlem"

Described as "London's miniature Harlem", the Shim Sham was central to black jazz music in London in the 1930s, with a reputation for being the first to receive music from across the Atlantic. Bottle parties offered opportunities for new musicians to play and improvised jazz jam sessions were known to take place in the venue. Police reports noted how music was key to the club, describing a small elevated bandstand and a curved bar central to the space, with room for dancing. Black British and African American performers utilised this performance space, which was in itself risky in an era of restrictions on American music performers in the UK. Together with the music, the Shim Sham was a space for radical politics, including pan-Africanism and anti-fascist meetings.

After the 1935 raid the venue re-opened as the Rainbow Roof, and was subject to further charges of unlicensed dancing and music in May and June 1936. In a climate of police surveillance, clubs such as the Shim Sham had to be resilient to change. However, it is clear that there was continued demand for these venues, and this drove them to reopen.

The Shim Sham's subversive mix of race, music, politics and sexual openness made it stand out to both the police and public. It can now be seen as a progressive venue that has since been championed as a black queer space and a key source of new music.

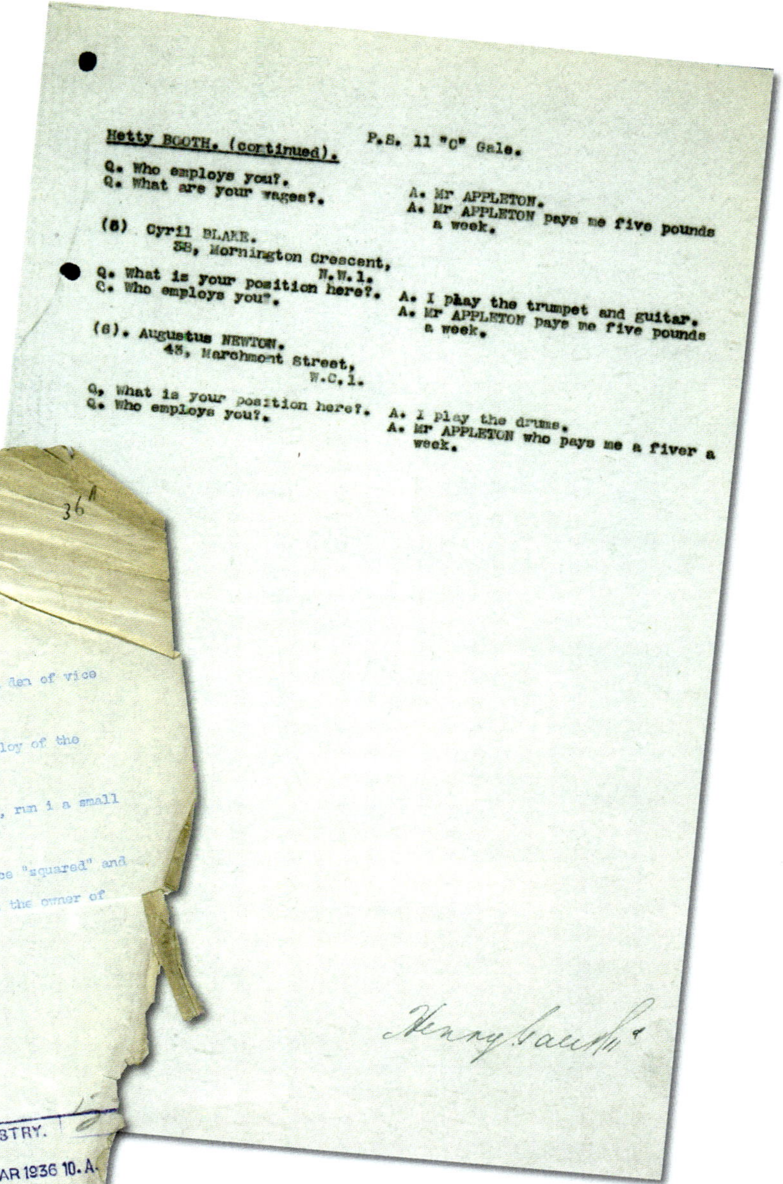

Hetty BOOTH. (continued). P.S. 11 "C" Gale.

Q. Who employs you?. A. Mr APPLETON.
Q. What are your wages?. A. Mr APPLETON pays me five pounds a week.

(5) Cyril BLAKE.
58, Mornington Crescent,
N.W.1.

Q. What is your position here?. A. I play the trumpet and guitar.
Q. Who employs you". A. Mr APPLETON pays me five pounds a week.

(6). Augustus NEWTON.
43, Marchmont Street,
W.C.1.

Q. What is your position here?. A. I play the drums.
Q. Who employs you?. A. Mr APPLETON who pays me a fiver a week.

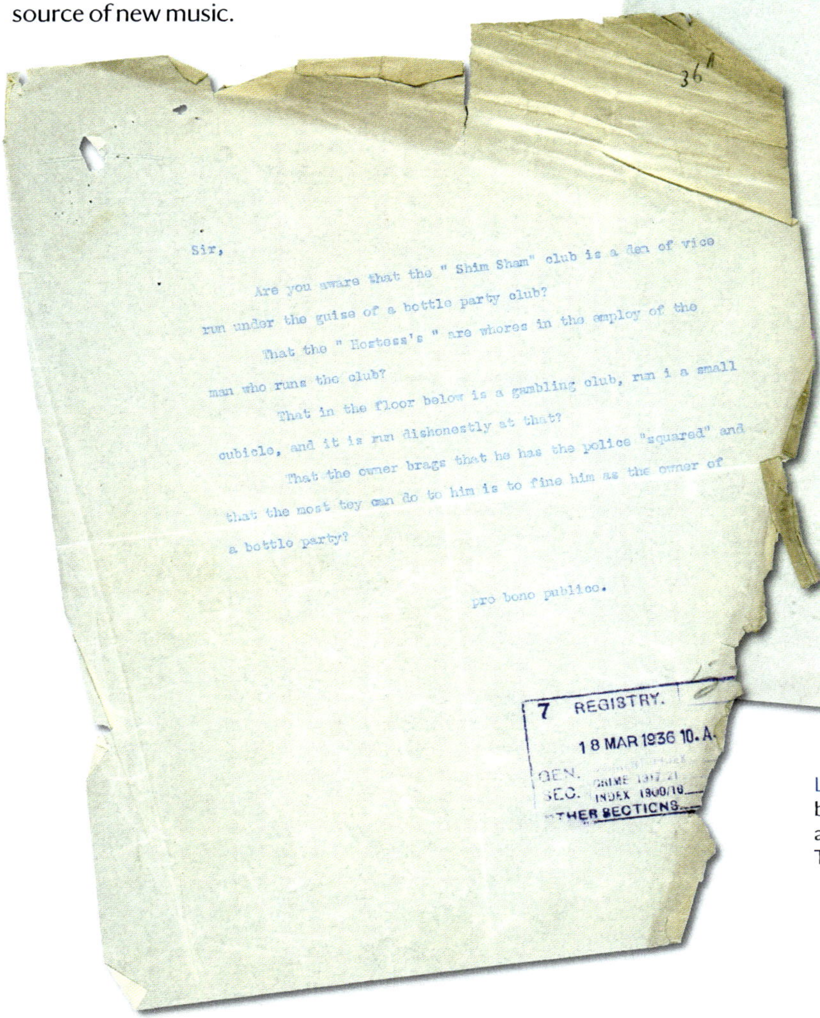

36

Sir,

Are you aware that the " Shim Sham" club is a den of vice run under the guise of a bottle party club?

That the " Hostess's " are whores in the employ of the man who runs the club?

That in the floor below is a gambling club, run i a small cubicle, and it is run dishonestly at that?

That the owner brags that he has the police "squared" and that the most tey can do to him is to fine him as the owner of a bottle party?

pro bono publico.

7 REGISTRY.
18 MAR 1936 10. A.
GEN. SEC. CRIME 1917 21 INDEX 1900/18
OTHER SECTIONS

Left Letter signed "pro bono public" in complaint about the Shim Sham, 1936. TNA: MEPO 2/4494

Above Members of the band being questions by police at the Shim Sham, 1935–1938. TNA: MEPO 2/449

# The Caravan, Covent Garden

"At above address there is the "Caravan" Club (?): only frequented by sexual perverts, lesbians and sodomites. It's absolutely a sink of iniquity."

Below left An invitation to the Caravan club. Words like "bohemian" and "unconventional" signalled that this space welcomed homosexual men, c.1934–1941.
TNA: MEPO 3/758

Below Letter from "Some ratepayers of Endell Street" to the Commissioner of Police, 1934.
TNA: MEPO 3/758

AFTER THE DAY'S ROUTINE SPEND YOUR EVENING AT

the caravan

81 ENDELL ST.

ENTRANCE IN COURT

(Corner of Shaftesbury Avenue, facing Princes Theatre)

Phone: Temple Bar 7665

*London's Greatest Bohemian Rendezvous*

*said to be the most unconventional spot in town*

ALL NIGHT GAIETY — Dancing to Charlie

PERIODICAL NIGHT TRIPS TO THE GREAT OPEN SPACES, INCLUDING THE ACE OF SPADES, ETC.

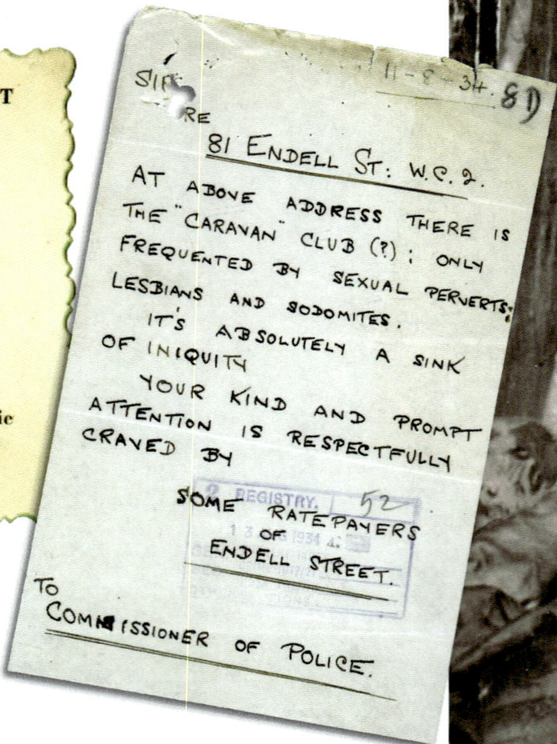

11-8-34. 81

SIR

RE
81 ENDELL ST: W.C. 2.

AT ABOVE ADDRESS THERE IS THE "CARAVAN" CLUB (?): ONLY FREQUENTED BY SEXUAL PERVERTS; LESBIANS AND SODOMITES. IT'S ABSOLUTELY A SINK OF INIQUITY

YOUR KIND AND PROMPT ATTENTION IS RESPECTFULLY CRAVED BY

SOME RATEPAYERS OF ENDELL STREET.

TO
COMMISSIONER OF POLICE.

The Caravan club, described in the 1930s as "London's greatest bohemian rendezvous", was a make-shift private members' club in the basement of 81 Endell Street, Soho. The club was run by Jack Neave, known as "Iron Foot Jack" and William Reynolds, known as "Billy". For the price of 1 shilling for members, or 1s 6d on the door, "all-night gaiety" could be enjoyed while dancing to the music of Charlie, the club's accordion player. In a society where gay men could be arrested, whipped and imprisoned for up to ten years if they were caught looking for partners on the street, commercial underground clubs in London's West End like the Caravan were vital places where men could freely meet, socialise and undertake relationships with other men.

Metropolitan Police files indicate that from October 1933 the Caravan club was kept under regular surveillance due to a number of complaints about the manner in which it was run. A note, signed anonymously by "Some rate

Police photograph of the interior of the Caravan club, 1934. TNA: DPP2/224

payers of Endell Street", describes the club as "an absolute sink of iniquity… frequented by sexual perverts, lesbians and sodomites". Police surveillance was often implemented in response to pressure from the public or organisations such as the London-based Public Morality Council (PMC), set up in 1899 to combat "vice and indecency". Agents from organisations such as these patrolled the streets and reported any behaviour that defied societal norms.

Police observed the Caravan club over a few weeks, watching from an unused part of the Shaftesbury Theatre and an old school. An hour-by-hour account of men entering and leaving the club on 11th October 1933 paid particular attention to any conversation that suggested the club was being used as a brothel or "disorderly house".

In the early hours of the morning of 25th August 1934, a number of plain-clothed policemen entered the club pretending to be visitors. Divisional Detective Inspector Clarence, the officer in charge of the raid, notes how he was able to introduce the officers without being noticed and describes the scene that greeted him:

> "The small dance floor was crowded and the number was too large to allow dancing properly. Men were dancing with men and women with women, a number of couples were simply standing still, and I saw couples wriggling their posteriors, and where I saw men together they had their hands on the others buttocks and were pressing themselves together. In fact all the couples I saw were acting in a very obscene manner."

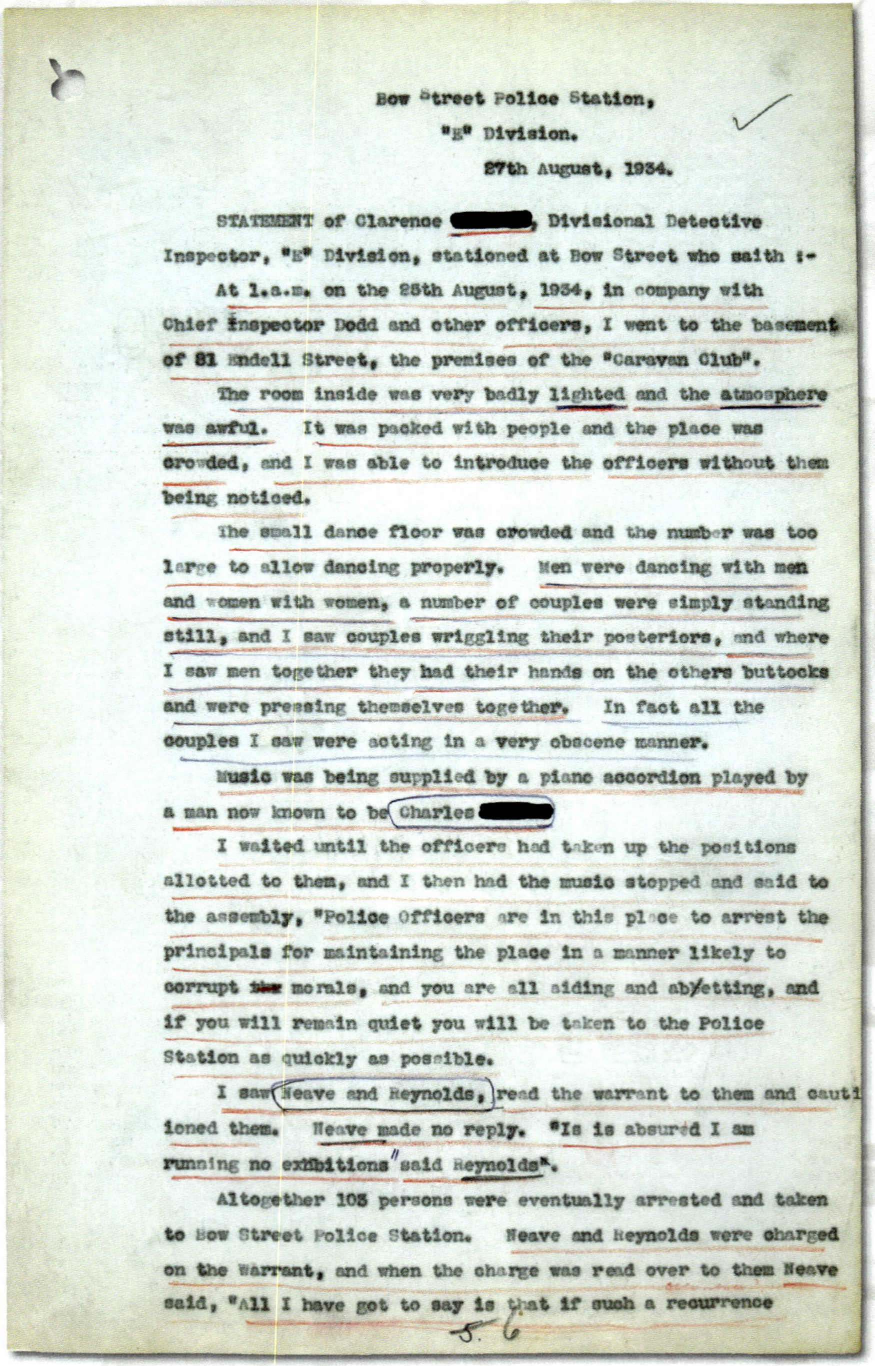

Bow Street Police Station,
"E" Division.
27th August, 1934.

STATEMENT of Clarence , Divisional Detective Inspector, "E" Division, stationed at Bow Street who saith :-

At 1.a.m. on the 25th August, 1934, in company with Chief Inspector Dodd and other officers, I went to the basement of 81 Endell Street, the premises of the "Caravan Club".

The room inside was very badly lighted and the atmosphere was awful. It was packed with people and the place was crowded, and I was able to introduce the officers without them being noticed.

The small dance floor was crowded and the number was too large to allow dancing properly. Men were dancing with men and women with women, a number of couples were simply standing still, and I saw couples wriggling their posteriors, and where I saw men together they had their hands on the others buttocks and were pressing themselves together. In fact all the couples I saw were acting in a very obscene manner.

Music was being supplied by a piano accordion played by a man now known to be Charles

I waited until the officers had taken up the positions allotted to them, and I then had the music stopped and said to the assembly, "Police Officers are in this place to arrest the principals for maintaining the place in a manner likely to corrupt morals, and you are all aiding and abetting, and if you will remain quiet you will be taken to the Police Station as quickly as possible.

I saw Neave and Reynolds, read the warrant to them and cauti ioned them. Neave made no reply. "Is is absurd I am running no exhibitions" said Reynolds".

Altogether 103 persons were eventually arrested and taken to Bow Street Police Station. Neave and Reynolds were charged on the Warrant, and when the charge was read over to them Neave said, "All I have got to say is that if such a recurrence

Left Statement by Divisional Detective Inspector Clarence, 1934. TNA: MEPO 3/758

Undercover investigation techniques were regularly adopted by the police to target clubs like the Caravan. These methods, particularly the use of agents provocateurs, led to growing public concern about the "moral corruption" of the police officers taking part. What is particularly striking in the reports of the Caravan raid is the emphasis on any behaviour viewed as "effeminate". Clarence, for example, states that a man was introduced as "Josephine" and describes how "a number of men had their faces powdered, their lips rouged and their eyebrows blackened". The focus on such behaviours suggests that the policing of the gay community relied heavily on stereotypes of queer men.

Clarence's report describes the dramatic moment when the police revealed themselves:

> "I waited until the officers had taken up their positions allotted to them, and I then had the music stopped and said to the assembly: "Police Officers are in this place to arrest principals for maintaining the place in a manner likely to corrupt morals, and you are all aiding and abetting, and if you will remain quiet you will be taken to the police station as quickly as possible".

Jack Neave's arrest is also recorded, along with his defence of the club: "I will admit that there is a variety of people who are eccentric ...I am willing to swear nothing suggestive or immoral has taken place". Clarence's statement ends with an account of Cyril de Leon approaching the inspector in an extraordinary act of resilience: "Well I don't mind this beastly raid, but I would like to know if you can let me have one of your nice boys to come home with. I am really good".

In the course of the raid 103 individuals, both men and women, were arrested and taken to Bow Street police station. During the arrest Cyril had to undergo the humiliating process of having his face tested for evidence of make-up with blotting paper. This practice was widely used to accuse gay men, again signifying how strong associations were held between certain characteristics and homosexuality.

> "At about 3am, the same day, at Bow Street Police Station I took pieces of blotting paper and rubbed them on the cheeks of Cyril de Leon; Frederick… (known to me as 'Josephine' a notorious sodomite): Eric…; Arthur…; William… and Frank …. All the pieces of blotting paper, which I produce, bear traces of rouge and all the men mentioned with the exception of [Frank] had their eyebrows plucked."

The ages and professions of those who visited the Caravan club were indicated on the list of persons committed for trial at the Central Criminal Court. Though most were young working class men – labourers, shop assistants or waiters – there were also examples of a wealthier clientele such as a school master and an engineer. The majority of these individuals were found "not guilty" on the condition that they never frequent such a club again, but the punishment for the owners was severe. Jack Neave and William Reynolds were found guilty of keeping a "disorderly house" described as "a place for people willing to pay for lewd, scandalous, bawdy and obscene performances and practices". Neave was sentenced to 20 months hard labour in prison, and Reynolds received 12 months.

The Caravan club trial incurred popular intrigue and was reported in public press. For those accused, exposure presented the added danger of being ostracised by friends, family and colleagues.

Among the police witness statements, reports and photographs of the raid and trial, there are personal letters that were used as evidence in court. These demonstrate a fascinating and unusual personal reflection on what it meant to be queer at the time.

The first letter, addressed from "Cyril" to "My darling Morris", was found at the scene. Cyril begins: "I was very disappointed that you were not coming to the club tonight", and describes "counting the hours until I could see you", signifying the importance of the Caravan club as a space where he could be himself; somewhere not just for casual sex, but where same-sex relationships were forged. The letter continues: "I only wish that I was going away with you, just you and I to eat, sleep and make love together,

Below Police photograph of the interior of the Caravan club, 1934. TNA: DPP2/224

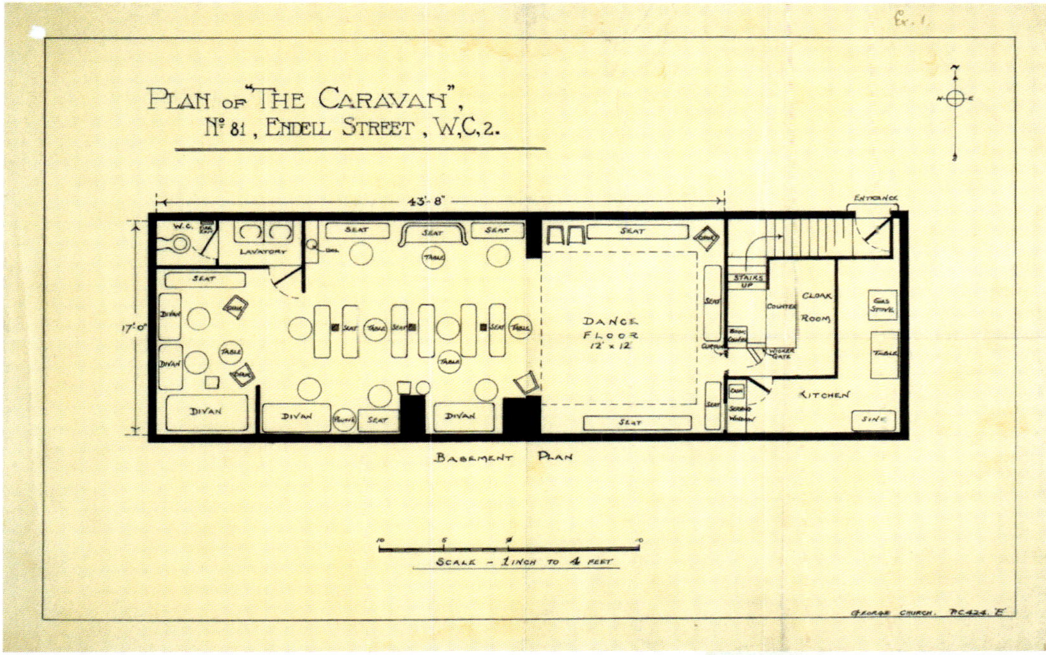


Above Police plan of "The Caravan", 1934.
TNA: DPP 2/224

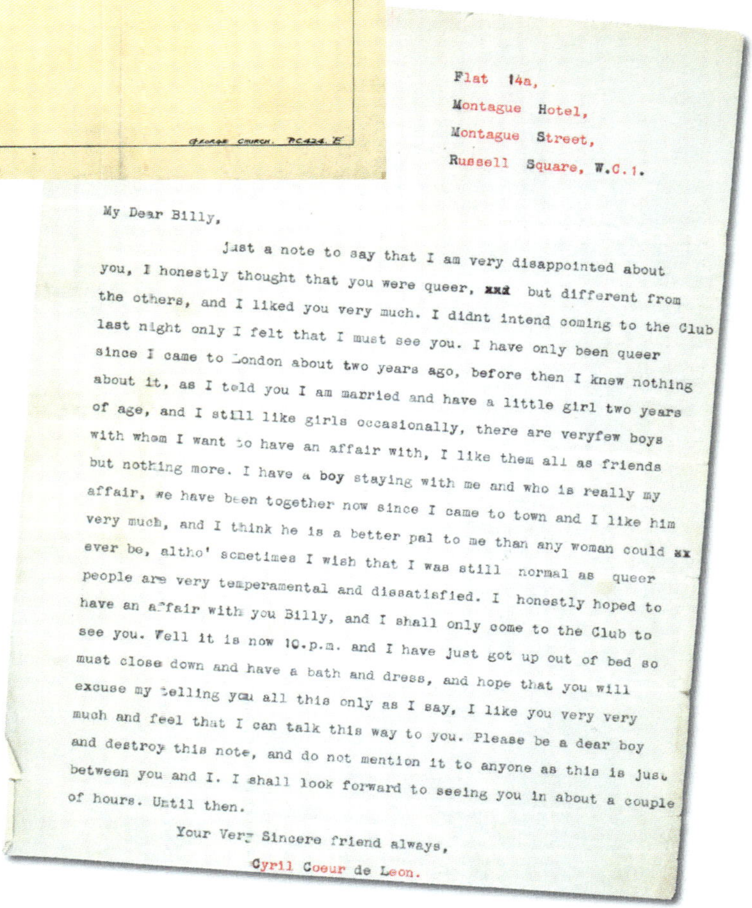

Flat 14a,
Montague Hotel,
Montague Street,
Russell Square, W.C.1.

My Dear Billy,

Just a note to say that I am very disappointed about you, I honestly thought that you were queer, xxx but different from the others, and I liked you very much. I didnt intend coming to the Club last night only I felt that I must see you. I have only been queer since I came to London about two years ago, before then I knew nothing about it, as I told you I am married and have a little girl two years of age, and I still like girls occasionally, there are veryfew boys with whom I want to have an affair with, I like them all as friends but nothing more. I have a boy staying with me and who is really my affair, we have been together now since I came to town and I like him very much, and I think he is a better pal to me than any woman could xx ever be, altho' sometimes I wish that I was still normal as queer people are very temperamental and dissatisfied. I honestly hoped to have an affair with you Billy, and I shall only come to the Club to see you. Well it is now 10.p.m. and I have just got up out of bed so must close down and have a bath and dress, and hope that you will excuse my telling you all this only as I say, I like you very very much and feel that I can talk this way to you. Please be a dear boy and destroy this note, and do not mention it to anyone as this is just between you and I. I shall look forward to seeing you in about a couple of hours. Until then.

Your Very Sincere friend always,

Cyril Coeur de Leon.

Right Letter from Cyril to Billy, 1934.
TNA: MEPO 3/758

perhaps when you are away you will think of me sometimes and even write me, I sincerely hope so." Found torn up under the divan with a powder puff, the note was retyped for the police file.

Another letter was found in a hotel bedroom on the Isle of Wight in the weeks following the raid. Written from Cyril to his dear friend Billy, the owner of the Caravan club, the letter describes how he has "only been queer since coming to London two years ago", and reveals he has a wife and a little girl. In addition to highlighting the social scene available to gay men in this era, it is revealing of "queer" identity at this time. The note ends with the powerful words "Please be a dear boy and destroy this note." Cyril was only too-aware of the implications if it was found.

# Billie's Club, Soho

Just around the corner from Endell Street was another prominent Soho members club on the queer scene at this time. Billie's Club was located on 6 Little Denmark Street, now Flitcroft Street, and opened in October 1935 run by club proprietor Billie Joyce.

Music and cabaret were central to Billie's, with prominent music hall artists of the era taking to the stage on Thursday and Saturday evenings. This venue actively attracted a queer audience, and the acts on stage reflected this, including openly queer music hall performers. The impressive club room hosted a dance floor and grand piano, in a more formal and less bohemian set up than the Caravan club. The rules of Billie's Club stated "The Club has been formed for the promotion of social, sporting and recreative intercourse, without any political object."

From May 1936 the property was under plain clothed police surveillance. Observations intensified between 31st October to 14th November 1936, and return visitors to the venue were noted by undercover police.

On 5th November 1936 PC Kenneth and PC George entered Billie's Club. Straight away both officers observed the majority of members were male. Kenneth noted "the majority of the males were of the nancy boy type and several had rouge and powder on their cheeks." Not only were the individuals perceived to be wearing make up but George noted "their hair was waved or dyed" and one individual was

Above Literature found in Billie's Club relating to music comedy performer Rosa Loader, 1937. TNA: CRIM 1/903

Interior photograph of Billie's Club, facing the dance floor, used as police evidence, 1937.
TNA: CRIM 1/903

highlighted as having pink nails. Police observations consistently related signs of female gender expression as a sign of homosexuality. One attendee commented "It's no good without a drag"; clearly many attendees relished the opportunity to dress up and explore their gender expression.

At 10pm it was announced queer musical hall artist Fred Barnes would sing some of his songs to the eager audience. Barnes was particularly well known for his signature song, "The Black Sheep of the Family". Police files collected various literature from performers of the era found in Billie's Club, hinting at the other types of music heard here, including the musical comedy actress Rosa Loader and performer George Barry, said to have "two voices in one".

## "They are not all bad"

Throughout the evening's performance the officers noted men disappearing into the toilets together. The dance floor was said to be full of couples pressed close together. PC Kenneth reported "A dance started with about 15 couples – all males – dancing… The dancing was exaggerated with motions of sexual intercourse standing up."

Kenneth observed "When I sat on one of the settees later, a male sitting there said to me: 'Are you queer, dear?' I said: 'What do you think?' He then said: 'Are you coming home with me?' I made an excuse that I had to meet someone else. Sergeant George and I left at 11.15pm."

On 14th November police raided Billie's Club. On entering the venue Chief Inspector Robert reported "a number of prisoners dancing, others sitting on settees caressing, and in a bedroom two men." As Robert read the warrant to Billie Joyce she responded with the words "They are not all bad, it is my job to control them." In nearly every instance the prisoners were noted to be powdered and rouged. Later that night 37 individuals were arrested and taken to Bow Street police station.

Those arrested during the raid were tried at the Central Criminal Court, on Tuesday 12th January 1936. The principal charges were keeping a disorderly house, and aiding and abetting. Even those just in attendance at Billie's Club were seen in the eyes of the law as aiding and abetting the venue, essentially criminalised for choice to love freely and socialise in queer spaces.

Uniquely, some letters survive that provide character testimonies relating to some of the arrested individuals. These come from relatives,

Below Character reference for prisoner George, 1937. TNA: CRIM 1/903

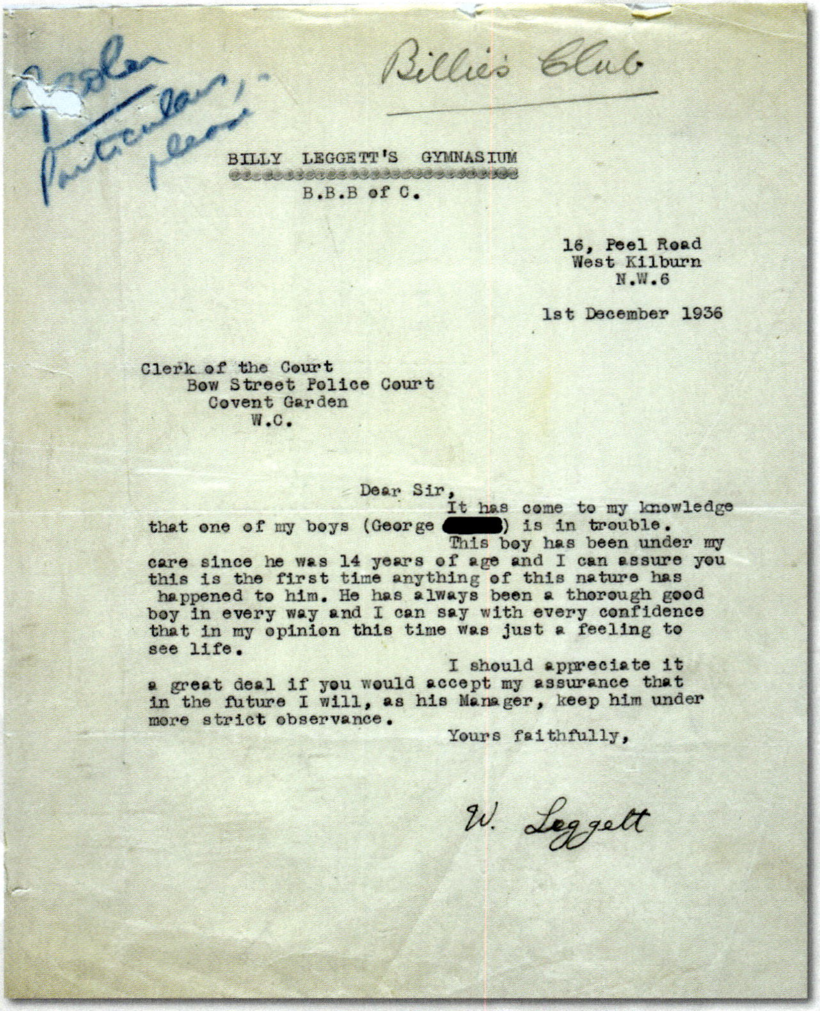

Billie's Club

BILLY LEGGETT'S GYMNASIUM
B.B.B of C.

16, Peel Road
West Kilburn
N.W.6

1st December 1936

Clerk of the Court
Bow Street Police Court
Covent Garden
W.C.

Dear Sir,

It has come to my knowledge that one of my boys (George ) is in trouble.

This boy has been under my care since he was 14 years of age and I can assure you this is the first time anything of this nature has happened to him. He has always been a thorough good boy in every way and I can say with every confidence that in my opinion this time was just a feeling to see life.

I should appreciate it a great deal if you would accept my assurance that in the future I will, as his Manager, keep him under more strict observance.

Yours faithfully,

W. Leggett

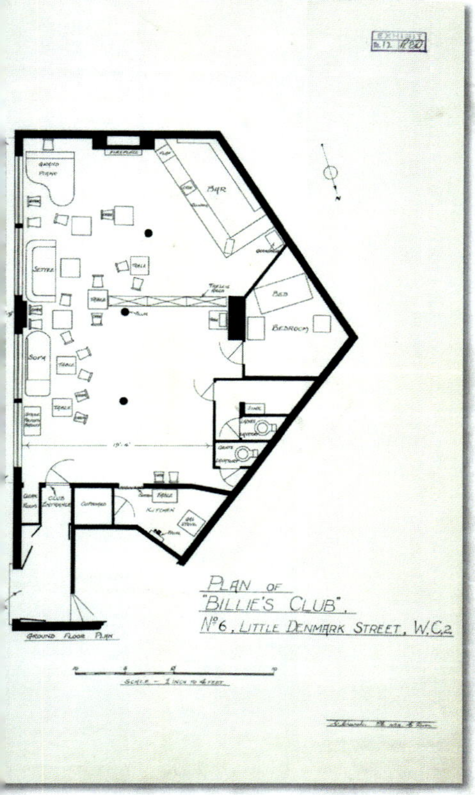


Above Police sketch of Billie's Club, No. 6 Little Denmark Street, 1936. TNA: DPP 2/355

most often fathers, while others provide references from employers. William Leggett, the owner of a gymnasium and employer of prisoner George, testifies to his work ethic, and closes the letter with the remarks "I trust you will be able to take the most lenient view possible of any breach of the law."

Charles was another of those arrested. Police reports chart Charles's experience of the club over multiple nights in 1936. Charles and his companion "were both highly powdered and painted and their eyebrows were made up. Their dancing consisted of suggestive movements and was exaggerated more than was necessary. [Charles and his companion] spoke in effeminate voices." On another occasion "A half-caste and Charles danced together alone about 9pm… They held each other very tightly at times. Their heads were well back when their stomachs were pressed together. After that dance, several people applauded it."

Part of the criminal proceedings surrounding the trial is a letter from Charles's father commenting on the character of his son, aged 18 years. Dated January 1937 this letter says that Charles has given his father "no trouble" and that "London is not suitable for him". There is a strong sense that it is the corrupting influence of London that is leading to Charles's queer identity. This reinforces the idea that London, and particularly Soho, were key to ideas of queer space and identity at this time. A particularly moving line ends the letter: "I know he will obey my wishes leave London seek a post in the country". As well as criminality, the pressures of family and jobs continued to affect queer people's lives. Frustratingly we do not know the end of Charles's story. Was he able to resist the pressure of his father and live his life freely?

Sentences for the individuals varied. George was found guilty of aiding and abetting, while proprietor Billie Joyce was charged with keeping a disorderly house and sentenced to 12 months in Wormwood Scrubs. The Music Hall artist Rich was found to have previous arrests for buggery and gross indecency, and was eventually sentenced to two years imprisonment, but ultimately recommended for deportation. Most individuals pleaded not guilty.

Like many of these records, the Central Criminal Court files give a great insight into what Soho, and London's queer scene, might have been like at this time. It illustrates the risks involved, but also the fun that could be had. This record particularly gives great details that evoke the atmosphere and music of the club, including photographs and plans of the interior. The numerous leaflets and booklets about the club and events hosted there create a picture of what it may have been like to be a patron.

The undercover policing of these spaces was controversial, and continued to be so until the 1960s. Home Secretary Roy Jenkins would note in January 1967, just prior to the change in law, that "while he was sure that the officers carrying out this very unpleasant work did so with great integrity, it was undeniable that they were exposed to great temptations and might in very rare cases be led into behaving as agents provocateurs." Jenkins inferred he would not unconditionally defend the practice of plain clothed officers. Policing methods often attracted press attention in this era, and in the 1960s the shift changed to uniformed police officers, with the recognition that the aim was to deter people from engaging in same sex relations, rather than what was sometimes perceived in the press as entrapment.

It's ironic that without the policing of these venues it is likely we would know even less about this pioneering queer clubs.

# Park House Private Ballroom, Holland Park

In 1932 the Park House Private Ballroom at 27 Holland Park Avenue was frequently rented out for drag dances by the ostentatious Lady Austin for gatherings of "Lady Austin's camp boys". While some of London's clubs of the era actively encouraged a queer clientele, other spaces, such as Park House, were only occasionally rented to members of this underground community.

Queer venues and gatherings provided spaces and opportunities for individuals to experiment with sexuality and gender expression in ways that were otherwise not socially accepted. These ballroom gatherings in particular were known as drag dances, where fancy dress costumes and clothing that questioned traditional gender expression was encouraged. At Holland Park Ballroom a large placard announced the fancy dress competition taking place, and fancy dress parades were also a common feature. This particular ballroom venue was part of a wider culture of queer spaces and organised events that spread through work networks, extending beyond Soho to the wider reaches of London.

## "Are you going to the 'Drag' tonight?"

On 13th December 1932 two undercover police offers were sent to investigate the premises on Holland Park Avenue. They entered the Mitre Public House, following in an individual with rouged lips, pencilled eyebrows and scented clothes who asked 'Are you going to the "Drag" tonight?' Subsequently, plain-clothed police officers PC Jack and PC Henry entered number 27, across the road from the bar, where they were introduced as "two camp boys and friends of mine". Each was then greeted with a kiss on the hand from a person wearing exaggerated makeup and an evening dress known as Lady Austin. Welcoming them, Austin remarked "Don't go and get too fruity yet".

The ballroom contained around 60 people. "One half of them were attired in evening dresses, the other half being dressed in lounge suits. All were male." The set-up was explained to the undercover officers; those wearing dresses were termed "Queenies" and those in lounge suits called "Kings". The officers each adopted a role and, in keeping with their disguise, pretended to be a couple. PC Jack stated 'For obvious reasons I acted as PC Henry's "Queenie"'. This illustrates the lengths police officers went to while investigating queer spaces.

In the course of such raids on queer spaces, police collected witness statements, reports and photographs. Objects were also gathered as evidence from the "crime" scenes, some of which survive in the records. Uniquely, this includes a red lounge suit worn by the "Kings", and this is still in existence in The National Archives' collection.

Both officers socialised, talked and danced with other attendees of the gathering. One individual explained "there were only five real women present and they were all Lesbians." PC Henry danced with a Queenie known as "The Bitch". During the dance Henry asked if everything was safe, and was told 'Safe dear, of course they can't touch us. If the "Bogies" or "Dicks" come, give a wrong name and address, I always do.'

Despite the police persecution of these spaces, it appears that they offered a sense of freedom

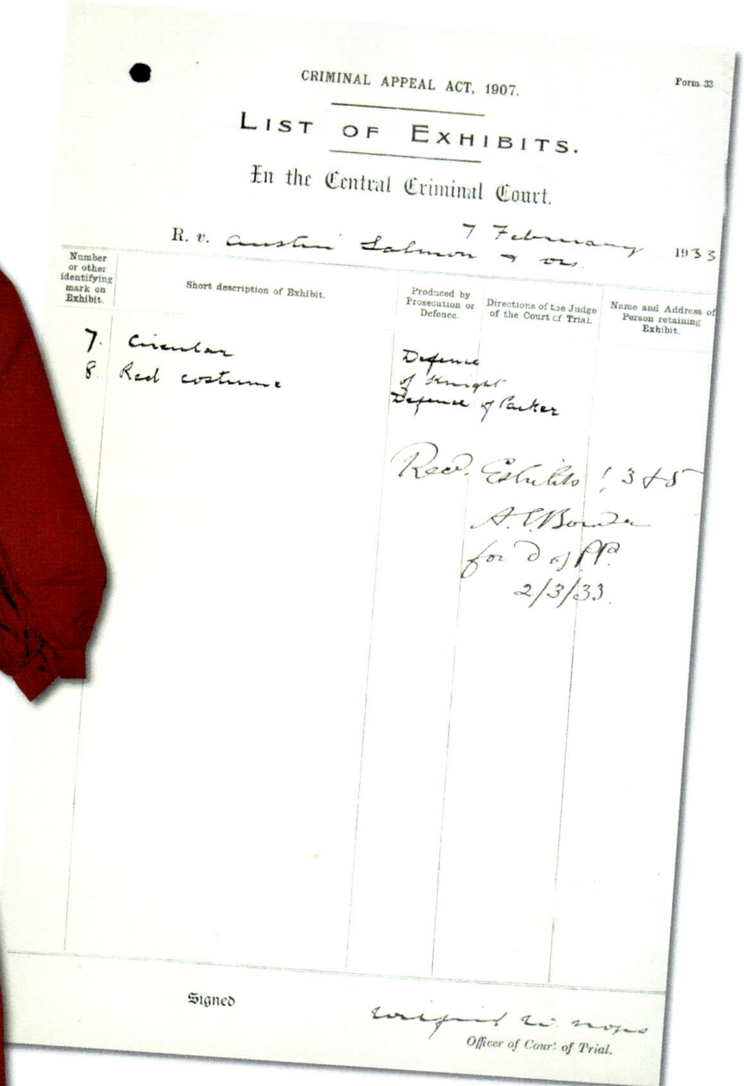
CRIMINAL APPEAL ACT, 1907. Form 33

LIST OF EXHIBITS.

In the Central Criminal Court.

R. v. Austin Salmon & ors. 7 February 1933

| Number or other identifying mark on Exhibit. | Short description of Exhibit. | Produced by Prosecution or Defence. | Directions of the Judge of the Court of Trial. | Name and Address of Person retaining Exhibit. |
|---|---|---|---|---|
| 7. | Circular | Defence of Knight | | |
| 8. | Red costume | Defence of Parker | | |

Recd Exhibits 1 3 + 5
[illegible]
for D of PP
2/3/33

Signed [illegible] Officer of Court of Trial.

Above List of exhibits taken as evidence at the Holland Park House raid, 1933. TNA: CRIM 1/638

Left A red silk pyjama suit produced as evidence, 1933. TNA: EXT 11/131

and safety to their patrons. Clearly, avoiding investigation was part of the queer way of life, and individuals developed techniques to try to evade police scrutiny.

These records hint at an accepted language for queer spaces, which the police engaged with. When PC Jack was asked if he had traded tonight yet he replied "Twice with my boy friend" and pointed to PC Henry, adapting to the language of the space. The officers watched couples sneak off to the toilets or gardens, and when the dance ended at 1am individuals paired off and left the property together.

## Working class queer culture

Not long afterwards, on December 20th, a waiter called William who worked and lived at the Balmoral Hotel was handed a flyer by a female friend, a chambermaid called Nancy. The handbill advertised a ball for hotel staff at the Park House Private Ballroom. The flyer summed-up the drag dance with the compelling phrase "Live, love and laugh". In this context, the reference to hotel staff seemed to suggest working class queer culture. This handbill would later appear as evidence in the criminal files.

Having received the flyer earlier in the day, William arrived at 27 Holland Park Avenue at 10:30pm, entering the large house from the busy road. While he claimed never to have visited the venue before, police statements note him as wearing make-up and having dyed hair; claims that he later denied. Officers' testimonies describe the scene that must have greeted William. When Sub-Divisional Inspector Frank arrived at the property, he spotted two men in the front garden, kissing and with their arms around each other, caught in the beam of a police torch.

Once again the ballroom was divided into Kings and Queenies. Lady Austin explained "We take it in turns; I was a Queenie last week." While the officers spoke to patrons in the ballroom, a guest called James asked "When did you discover that you were like it. I did two years ago. Other people would sympathise with us if they knew and knew we couldn't help it." As these lines show, police observations of queer spaces often reveal personal reflections on identity and sexuality.

At 11:25pm the Chief Inspector and other officers entered the ballroom. He notes "I waited till all the officers had got round the room. Then I announced we were police officers. I had the band stopped. I then shouted out, 'I want Lady Austin and Betty'."

Prisoner Austin said, "I am her ladyship. Betty is not here."

As the premises were raided Lady Austin defended the dance, and when the police warrant was read out, said "Surely only members of our cult are here. What harm are we doing? You don't understand our love." Police enquired what Austin meant by "members of our cult", "Why Lady Austin's camp boys of course." Austin claimed they knew each other from Betty's at Baker Street. This response is clearly illustrative of a wider network of queer clubs and friendship networks in London at this time.

Austin explained the venue was run for love not profit. "How difficult is it? You don't understand. We don't like women, a drag is a dance without women and give and take is between ourselves. Oh, dear, this trouble would be obviated if they made our love legal." It would take a further thirty years for homosexual acts in private to be legalised in England and Wales.

The police recorded the names of "all men dressed as women", and took all those arrested to the police station. In the ballroom and cloakroom police found powder puffs, lipsticks, and ladies' knickers and shoes, many of which were taken as evidence.

At the trial Lady Austin was one of the foremost individuals to be found guilty, with the principal charges of "conspiracy to corrupt morals" and "keeping a disorderly house".

People owning and running properties such as this were seen much more harshly in the eyes of the law. Simply by living their lives the way they wished to, these men risked arrest and prosecution, which could lead to jail sentences and years of hard labour.

Above Handbill advertising a ball for 'hotel staff' taken as evidence, 1933. TNA: CRIM 1/638

# Tackling Prejudice and Celebrating with Pride

Rachael Lennon, National Trust

In December 2016, the National Trust launched *Prejudice and Pride,* a year-long exploration of LGBTQ+ heritage across England, Wales and Northern Ireland. 50 years after the partial decriminalisation of homosexual acts, celebrations and commemorations are taking place to mark the lives of people who challenged conventional notions of gender and sexuality.

LGBTQ+ heritage is an important part of all our history and, like today, many National Trust places were the homes and workplaces of members of an LGBTQ+ community.

Events will be taking place across National Trust properties, from Kingston Lacy in Dorset to Beningbrough Hall in North Yorkshire. For the first time, the Trust will have a widespread, national presence at Pride festivals. We are publishing new guidebooks and online resources and releasing a podcast series to shine a spotlight on these histories.

Some of our stories are relatively well known and some have remained hidden until now.

Kingston Lacy was dramatically shaped by the vision of William John Bankes. In 1841 Bankes was forced to flee England to avoid prosecution for same-sex acts, and, if found guilty, could have faced the death penalty. From his exile in Europe, Bankes sent back a vast collection of art as well as minute directions as to the development of his home. No longer free to visit Kingston Lacy, his passion for the place continued until his death in Venice in 1855. This year, Kingston Lacy will begin to share the story of Bankes' persecution and exile and invite queer voices to enrich the contemporary relevance and significance of this story.

The relationship between Vita Sackville West and Virginia Woolf was immortalised in the passionate letters they exchanged, as well as Virginia Woolf's gender-queer novel *Orlando*. The character of Orlando was heavily inspired by Vita Sackville West and takes place at a Knole-like estate, spanning 400 years of the history of the house.

Above Vita Sackville-West's copy of Virginia Woolf's *Orlando* © National Trust Images

Right Virginia Woolf by Lenare © National Trust/ John Hammond

In a letter to Virginia Woolf, Vita Sackville West wrote:

> "I am reduced to a thing that wants Virginia. I composed a beautiful letter to you in the sleepless nightmare hours of the night, and it has all gone: I just miss you, in a quite simple desperate human way."

The couple developed their relationship at Knole, Virginia and Leonard's home at Monks House and Vita and Harold's home at Sissinghurst. Each of these places will mark the 50 year anniversary through *Prejudice and Pride* commemorations. A copy of *Orlando*, signed by Virginia Woolf to Eddy Sackville West, was acquired by the National Trust through the programme and will be marked with events and screenings of the 1992 movie at Knole in June 2017.

Nearby, at Smallhythe Place, an exhibition will take place to explore the life and arts of Edy Craig and her two partners, Christabel Marshall (aka Christopher Marie St John) and Clare (Tony) Atwood. In Shropshire, Hanbury Hall have invited a number of artists to create contemporary responses to a dramatic set of murals which include depictions of Achilles and his lover Patroclus.

In Hackney, the Tudor mansion Sutton House is hosting four seasons of events to showcase works by LGBTQ+ artists, to explore activism, unpick fluid identities in *Alice in Wonderland*, and commemorate vanishing LGBTQ+ spaces in London. The property's first gender neutral toilet will be launched with a sound installation in what is thought to be the oldest toilet in Hackney.

*Prejudice and Pride* will help to demonstrate how deeply and widely LGBTQ+ heritage goes back into our shared history. We are working with a number of communities, artists and creative practitioners to breathe life into our places, collections and stories.

Left Sutton House Queered Launch © Eli Beristain

The legacy of the programme will grow in years to come as we continue to research and better understand these histories; as we invite in Stonewall and other partners to reflect on our work, and as we partner with Historic England to relist buildings in our care to stronger reflect their LGBTQ+ heritage.

We are committed to ensuring that the National Trust protects and shares the wonderful places in its care for ever and for everyone. Bestselling author, and *Prejudice and Pride* contributor, Sarah Waters has reflected on the programme:

> "These days we can all be a bit bolder about exploring and enjoying the UK's rich heritage of sex and gender diversity. And I'd argue that without an awareness of that heritage our experience of certain National Trust properties is incomplete."
>
> *National Trust* magazine, January 2017